'Play is at the heart of science, the a
architecture – in short the world we live in. We all learn
through play. Yet, for some reason play gets downgraded
as trivial. Perhaps that's because we love it. This book
puts play where it belongs: at the heart of our lives.'
– Michael Rosen, writer and broadcaster

'The best kind of books offer the reader an adventure within
their pages and the best kind of adventure is one that leads
to something new. Georgina has skilfully created a wealth
of fantastic fresh ideas that act like a much-needed map
guiding us towards a deeper understanding of who the
unique child truly is and how play, with all its magic, can
show them the joyful gift of being a reader and a writer.'
**– Greg Bottrill, childhood advocate and
author of *Can I Go and Play Now?***

'Well done Georgina, another brilliant book for playful
parents! It's so refreshing to see lots of ways to practise
those essential early reading and writing skills in fun and
active ways! This will be such a helpful guide for so many
of us wanting to give our children the best start in life.'
– Claire Russell, Founder of playHOORAY!

'When I was reading this book what struck me immediately
was the sheer depth of Georgina's knowledge on how to
support reluctant readers. Since being lucky enough to
have 'early access', I have found myself recommending this
book to other professionals, parents and carers alike!'
**– Dr Helen Ross, Trustee of the British Dyslexia Association,
dyslexic dyslexia expert and educational consultant**

'This is a unique and seemingly never-ending supply of fun-filled
ideas to develop our children as readers and writers. Durrant has
cleverly provided us with the go-to manual for those who wish to
enthuse and empower children in their literacy journey.'
**– Chris Dyson, Headteacher, Parklands Primary School, author of
*Parklands: A School Built on Love***

How to Boost
READING & WRITING
Through Play

Fun Literacy-Based Activities for Children

Georgina Durrant

ILLUSTRATED BY CHRISTOPHER BARNES
FOREWORD BY THEO PAPHITIS

Jessica Kingsley Publishers
London and Philadelphia

First published in Great Britain in 2023 by Jessica Kingsley Publishers
An imprint of Hodder & Stoughton Ltd
An Hachette Company

1

A CIP catalogue record for this title is available from the British Library
and the Library of Congress

ISBN 978 1 83997 456 4
eISBN 978 1 83997 457 1

Printed and bound by CPI Group (UK) Ltd, Croydon, CR0 4YY

Jessica Kingsley Publishers' policy is to use papers that are natural,
renewable and recyclable products and made from wood grown
in sustainable forests. The logging and manufacturing processes
are expected to conform to the environmental regulations
of the country of origin.

Jessica Kingsley Publishers
Carmelite House
50 Victoria Embankment
London EC4Y 0DZ

www.jkp.com

To my brilliant husband for being my biggest ally. And to our children, who have made me the luckiest mummy in the world.

CONTENTS

. . . .

FOREWORD

Author's note

Theo Paphitis, the successful dyslexic entrepreneur, has kindly provided the following forewords for this book. The first has used a spellchecker and the second is Theo's original writing – we think this highlights that ambition and success in life is in no way limited by reading and writing skills. We hope that by using this book the children you look after or work with learn to have fun with words, and find creative ways to develop their literacy

Spellchecked

I like to think that dyslexia is a different way of thinking – throughout school, my brain would often understand that I needed to find a solution, but couldn't do it the way everybody else was doing it, but that's okay. Identifying dyslexia is the first step, and then you can understand how to use it to your advantage.

I would find workarounds to get the answer and my mind would be going all over the place, but I would get there. Because it was slow and methodical it meant I had to work harder than everyone else and by the time I got to the big bad world I could look at a problem and I was already gearing up to find a solution.

I firmly hold the belief that dyslexic people have an uncanny ability to problem-solve, visualize, understand complex issues and find workarounds that I've never seen before in another group of people

With our understanding of dyslexia evolving all the time and as a result of improvements in technology, it is now even easier to find ways to identify and work successfully with those with dyslexia.

It is important that we identify and work with those who have dyslexia from an early age so we can truly harness their potential, and out-of-the-box resources, such as this book, are a fantastic example of how we can do just that.

Theo Paphitis, dyslexic entrepreneur

Now...without spellcheck

I like 2 think that dyslexia is a difrent way of thinking - thruout school, my brain wud often understand that I needed to find a solootion, but coodn't do it the way evrybody else was doing it, but that's ok. Identifying dislexia is the 1st step, and then you can understand how to use it to your advarntidge.

I would find workrounds to get the final arnsir, and my mind would be going all over the plaice, but I would get there. Becoz it was slow and methodical it meant I had to work harder than evryone else and by the time I got to the big bad world, I cud look at a problem and I was allreddy geered up to find a solootion.

I firmly hold the beleef that dislexic peeple have an uncanni abiliti to problem-solve, visulise, understand complex isues and find workrounds that I've never seen befor in anotha group of people.

With our understanding of dislexia evollving all the time and as a reesult of improvments in technology, it is now eeven easier than ever to find ways to identify and work sucsessfully with those with dislexia.

It is important that we identify and work with those who have dislexia from an early age so we can truly harness their potenshall, and out-of-the-box resorces, such as this book, are a fantastick exarmple of how we can do just that.

Theo Paphitis, dyslexic entrepreneur

ACKNOWLEDGMENTS

I'd like to thank Jessica Kingsley Publishers for inviting me to pitch a proposal for this, my second book. Thanks, in particular, to my wonderful editor Emily, who is such a huge support and is always open to listening to my ideas (even when I change them).

Thank you to every single person who bought my first book, *100 Ways Your Child Can Learn Through Play*, and shared lovely reviews and photographs with me. It has meant the world to know that my book has been helpful for children, and the feedback provided me with the motivation to write this book.

Once again, thank you to everyone who follows my blog (The SEN Resources Blog), for reading my posts and sharing them. You were the ones at the start of my writing journey, enabling me to be in a position to pitch my first book. And thanks to your continued support I have been able to write this one too.

I would like to thank my parents for their continued encouragement and guidance, in particular my mum, who diligently reads and checks every draft I write.

Thank you to my children for being my biggest cheerleaders, telling everyone they know that their mummy is an author and often strongly hinting to people that they should buy my books (I think they are definitely responsible for selling a few copies).

Thanks to my brilliant brother and best friend Chris, for once again agreeing to draw all the beautiful illustrations for my book. Apologies for the short deadline!

Finally, thank you to my amazing husband who has helped me find the time to write this book, despite our lives being incredibly busy.

PREFACE

. . . .

Making reading and writing enjoyable has been a huge part of my life of late – not just as a parent navigating the temporary home learning of the pandemic like so many others, but as a former teacher, special educational needs and disabilities coordinator (SENDCO) and most recently a private tutor for children with special educational needs and disabilities (SEND).

I wrote my first book, *100 Ways Your Child Can Learn Through Play*, published in June 2021, to empower parents and teachers to embrace play-based learning and help children develop important skills. I wanted them to step away from the guilt that their children were 'just playing' and to be filled with confidence in the skills their children could hone while having fun. Skills developed included everything from fine motor skills, speech and language to literacy and numeracy.

And on the back of the success of my first book, I wanted to go one step further and focus more specifically on the area that I see children regularly struggle with (and as a result sometimes dislike), and that's reading and writing.

I'm sure I'm not alone when I say that I've seen the point at which that spark goes, and children who have successfully learned how to read and write basic words and sentences become disillusioned, unmotivated and unhappy writing and reading.

Therefore, the aim of this book is not just to boost children's reading and writing but also to help them fall back in love with it. I want to help relight that spark that they may have had when they arrived in school, fresh faced, with baggy uniform and a pristine book bag aged four, ready to learn.

And, if they have never enjoyed reading and writing, I aim to give you as parents and teachers some fresh, new ideas that will hopefully be your 'way in' to help them love it.

As a former SENDCO, I know that for many children it's not simply that they lack motivation, but that reading and writing are inherently more challenging for them. In fact, they may be putting in ten times more effort each lesson than their peers, but not reaping the same progress. Or they may have 'given up' as a result. This could be due to a reading difficulty such as dyslexia (diagnosed or not) or another SEND. With this firmly in mind, I've tried to create activities that are suitable (and in my experience work) at supporting *all* children, including those with SEND, to find success in reading and writing. I've also attempted to address and find solutions to the most common barriers that children face with their reading and writing.

I'm also acutely aware of the impact the pandemic has had (and as I write this, is still having) on children, and the need to find ways to help get children's reading and writing 'back on track' while still nurturing their emotional well-being. And that is another reason I'm so passionate about the power of play. Play can be wonderful for children's mental health and well-being, and happy, relaxed children are more able to learn. Children haven't just missed out educationally due to the pandemic, they also need to 'catch up' on lost play.

In my experience, children who enjoy and achieve at reading and writing find other subjects easier as they go through school. Reading and writing are also not separate entitites, but interwoven into every subject they learn. For example, to be successful at science children will need to be able to read questions, write predictions and explain results. As a former secondary school science teacher, I've taught many children whose scientific knowledge was exceptional, but due to their literacy skills they couldn't achieve the grades they deserved.

Just as literacy is important to other subjects, other skills are also important for literacy. For example, to be physically able and comfortable to write, children need to have good fine and gross motor skills. Fine motor skill activities are those that develop the tiny muscles in the fingers and hands that are needed to learn to write and complete other tasks, such as using a zip when getting dressed. Gross motor skills are those that use the bigger muscles. Activities such as jumping or throwing use gross motor skills. Gross motor skills are equally important for writing as these muscles help with postural control and being able to sit comfortably to write. Once children have learned the basics of reading and writing, it can still be important to continue to develop these skills through practice. What made my first book, *100 Ways Your Child Can Learn Through Play*, appealing to parents and teachers was the handy tick box at the bottom of each activity that highlighted which key skills children are developing through play. In response to this feedback, I've kept the boxes for this book too, as a way of reminding parents and teachers that children are not only developing their literacy skills with these activities, but a whole host of other skills too.

I hope you find my book useful and that you dip in and out of it for ideas. Ultimately, I hope it helps children, of all abilities, to discover or rediscover a love of reading and writing through play.

INTRODUCTION

You have cracked it! The children you're teaching, or parenting, have learned how to read and write, they know their phonics sounds and they can read their reading books in their book bag. The job is done...but wait...why is it still difficult to get them to read and write? Why don't they *want* to do it? Why is reading becoming a chore for them? And why do they only want to write the shortest amount possible? This is a question I get asked time and time again and my answer might surprise you – let them play! Now I don't mean just scrap the reading and writing and send them out to play instead. No. What I mean is, remember *who* you're trying to get to read and write. Think of your clientele. These aren't mini adults who are happy to sit at a desk (I suppose you may ask, are adults happy to sit at a desk? But that's for a different time!), these are children. Children love to run, jump, dance, create, make, investigate and imagine. We need to step into their world and make reading and writing part of it. Weave it into their play and show them that reading and writing are fun. As the phrase goes 'if you can't beat them, join them' and this is true in this situation. For children, sitting at a desk is never going to beat the appeal of playing. So don't always choose to fight a losing battle. Instead, join them and take the reading and writing with you.

Most of the activities in this book don't involve sitting at a table with pencils, paper or books. Instead, when you flick through the activities you'll see water balloons, role-play, ice and even some monsters made from pasta. I completely understand that this may not fit with your view of how children, especially those over five years old, should read and write. Many of us were brought up to believe that all learning happened formally, at a desk with a book. It may also not fit in neatly with the current curriculum. So, I invite you to let me persuade you that sometimes the learning of reading and writing can happen through play. Embrace the activities, give them a go, and see for yourselves the positive effect play can have, not just on learning to read and write but on children's self-esteem and view of literacy. I would also wager that the bond you'll create with the children in your home or school will flourish as a result.

As a former SENDCO, I know that reading and writing also don't come easily to many children (or adults) and that there are many barriers that children face when developing these skills. This could be due to a specific SEND such as dyslexia. And while play-based approaches aren't going to diminish the reading difficulty, they can be a more accessible way of learning to read and write, and may take the pressure off children.

Barriers to reading and writing

I want to first unpick the barriers to reading and writing with you. Play is important, but we need to be aware of the barriers that children can face when reading and writing (of which there can be many) in order to support children in being successful. The barriers vary from those that we may be able to easily sort, such as lighting and comfort, to those that are more intrinsic, such as a specific SEND or having English as an additional language. Consider these barriers when facilitating the activities in this book and when looking at children's overall experience of reading and writing, and think how you can support them. I cannot claim to be an expert in all the barriers to reading and writing, but I will now look at the biggest barriers that I have found (in my experience) and at some suggestions of what we can do to help.

Self-esteem

It is understandable that children may not want to read and write if they don't feel successful at it. It is hard to keep trying at something if you're getting 'knocked back'.

Spelling ability can have a huge impact on children's self-esteem. I've known very articulate children not wanting to write more than a short, snappy sentence about a subject they are passionate about, simply because they knew they could not spell some of the words and it was too upsetting to get spellings wrong and have them corrected. Children also compare themselves to their peers and will soon become aware if they are finding spelling harder than their friends.

Reading fluency is another area I've witnessed having a big effect on children's self-esteem. I explain reading fluency as when you are able to read as if you are talking, at a 'normal' speed and without regular pauses to work out the words. It takes a lot of confidence to read out loud, especially if you find it difficult. And for this reason, children who struggle with reading fluency often, quite simply (and completely understandably), don't want to put themselves in that situation.

How can we help?

- Find engaging ways to enable children to practise and find success with their reading and writing (play-based activities for example).
- Build reading and writing into everyday life (see Chapter 5 for ideas).
- Ensure that children's spelling ability is not compared to others in front of them.
- Avoid choosing children to read out loud difficult texts if it will be detrimental to their self-esteem. Perhaps discuss with the child quietly beforehand, asking them if they are okay to read that day. Try giving them time to practise what they will be reading beforehand too.

How we frame literacy

There's a real danger that we, unintentionally, frame reading and writing negatively and as a chore. For example, just simple comments and questions, which I'm guilty myself of having said as a parent, such as, 'We need to read that reading book in your folder again tonight, don't we?' How on earth does that create a love of reading? All I've done in that moment is made my child realize that not only do I think their reading book is a chore, but they should too. When in reality, it's not; I love listening to my children read. It's just that, through no fault of our own, we lead very busy lives and are prone to throw-away comments that unfortunately stick. Children's views and opinions at a young age are massively influenced and shaped by their parents and caregivers. It is vital that we don't make them think that listening to them read is a 'job'.

How can we help?

- Prioritize reading – give it the value it deserves and be positive about it. Pass on a positive image to them.
- Whether at school or at home, 'sell' writing to children positively.
- Some parents will also have had negative experiences with reading and writing and may find it difficult themselves. I can't claim to be an expert on this, but if this is you, my advice would be *not* to pretend to your child that you love reading and writing, but instead be truthful. Explain that you find it difficult and show them there's no shame in this. Learning things together can also be hugely positive.

Difficulty level

We must make sure that the book or writing task is not too difficult or too easy. Teachers are very skilled at this and, as parents, it is important that we ask for their guidance when we are unsure.

Giving children a book to read, for example, that is far too difficult will only demotivate a child, while giving them a book that's too easy may make children view reading as boring and repetitive.

We also need to think about the content of the books, ensuring they are age appropriate and not too 'babyish' or 'boring' if a child is reading at a lower reading age than their chronological age.

How can we help?

- Ensure that everyone who reads with the child knows their reading level (to some extent) so books can be chosen to match it.
- If the child's reading age does not match their chronological age, choose books that have a suitable interest level as well as reading level. There are bookshops that enable you to select books that are at a child's reading age and interest age.

Special educational needs and disabilities (SEND)

There are many types of SEND, both diagnosed and undiagnosed, that can make reading and writing more challenging for a child. A paragraph in this book won't be able to do this topic justice or cover all the specific types of SEND. Most people probably know now about the impact that reading difficulties such as dyslexia can have on reading, writing and spelling. But it's important to remember other types of SEND can also have a profound impact. Speech, language and communication needs (SLCN), for example, can make reading and writing more challenging due to the child's potential difficulty with phonological awareness. SEND that affects children's motor skills, such as cerebral palsy, may make writing more challenging due to difficulties with postural control and fine motor skills.

I must point out that we must be very careful not to deny children the pleasure of reading and writing due to their SEND – a non-verbal or pre-verbal child, for example, may still be very capable of reading, and a child who can't hold a pen is equally able to write. It's our job to strip down the barriers to make reading and writing accessible for all.

How can we help?

- Remember that each child with SEND is unique and it is important to fully understand not only their diagnosis and its impact on reading and writing but also the child's personal experiences. What are they good at? What do they find difficult? How would they like us to make it easier for them? What technology may be useful (see Chapter 5)?

- If you think a child may have an undiagnosed SEND, speak to your GP and school SENDCO.
- Ensure excellent communication between school, any external services, families and the child, passing information, advice, tips and things that have worked between all parties.
- Put in place recommendations of adjustments to help the child, reviewing and evaluating their impact regularly.

Time

Time can be a barrier for reading and writing in many different ways – whether it be the wrong time, too much time, too little time or the pressure of time.

By the wrong time, I mean being aware that children (just like us) aren't always in the right mindset for writing and reading – just as I had to be stress free and relaxed and had to pick an optimum time to write this book. Just because we, as adults, have designated some time to reading, doesn't mean that the child is feeling at their best for it too.

Some children may need more time to read and absorb information or write sentences than others and we must always bear this in mind and plan for it. It must be incredibly frustrating to be given insufficient time to read or write something, especially if you know you are able to do it given the time.

Many children dislike the pressure of time when reading and writing, and having a reminder of how much time is left to complete something can put unnecessary pressure on some. Likewise, for some children, being aware of how much time is left on a task before they move on can be helpful.

How can we help?

- Give children enough time to read and write.

- Give them some choice over when they read and write. This is particularly important at home when reading their reading books from school or when writing their homework.
- Be guided by the children; if it is apparent that time pressures have a negative impact on their reading and writing, don't use timers, countdowns and so on.

Difficulty concentrating

Children can find it difficult to concentrate on reading and writing for many reasons. It could be the environment that is proving too distracting and/or they have a specific SEND such as attention deficit hyperactivity disorder (ADHD) that may make it intrinsically harder for them.

In terms of environmental factors, noise, warmth, comfort and lack of space can all have an impact on children's ability to concentrate.

When setting writing tasks, either at home or school, think about how you would set yourself up if you had to write something for a period of time. Would you grab a cup of tea, clear some space on a tabletop, sit on a comfy desk chair, use your best pen? What else would you do? And whatever it is, minus perhaps the cup of tea, see if you can allow children similar luxuries. Are they thirsty, are they warm enough, is the desk/table at the right height, is the sun in their eyes, are they hungry, is their pencil sharp? And ask them what they need to write more comfortably. All these simple checks might be frustrating and delay the start of the task, but they are so important for enabling children to gain success in reading and writing and to see it in a positive light. You'll also find that children will get quicker at these checks and take control of them themselves over time, providing them with a toolkit to ensure their own well-being when writing.

The same goes for reading. Picture yourself when you read. Do you sit on a hard chair with your feet on the floor? Or do you curl up on a comfy sofa (or even better, a deckchair in the sun?) Do you listen to music? Let children experience the same pleasure of being curled up with a book!

How can we help?

- Ensure basic (yet important) needs are met first – comfort, safety, food, water, warmth.
- Make the environment as free from noise distractions as you can.
- Understand any SEND and put in place any adjustments needed.
- Use any additional resources needed such as ear defenders or background music.
- Create an area inviting for reading and writing (see Chapter 5).

Lack of representation in books

Children need to 'see' themselves in the books they read. They need to feel accepted. If a neurodivergent child, for example, never sees or reads of a neurodivergent person in a book, or never reads a book written by a neurodivergent author, they may feel that books and writing are not meant for them. The same goes for disabilities, skin colour, religion and so on. And importantly, when books do represent children, they must not be written from a deficit perspective.

How can we help?

- Make sure there's representation for all children in the books they are surrounded by.
- Include books written by a diverse range of authors.

Comprehension

Successful reading isn't just about being able to read words in a row as part of a sentence. It is vital that children are able to also understand what they have read. Some dyslexic children I have taught, for example, were excellent readers but when asked about the text they read, they had little recollection as to what happened. They may have been concentrating so hard on reading the individual words that it was too difficult to also process what was happening in the text.

Comprehension can also be made more difficult if children have made errors when reading a text, as it will make less sense to them if some of the words were misread. We also need to be aware that children who have difficultly writing may find that their comprehension orally is fantastic, but they struggle to get their ideas on paper.

How can we help?

- Develop children's reading ability through regular practice to reduce reading errors. Multi-sensory play with key words (see Chapter 1) can be helpful for some children to help them remember key words.
- Discuss books together while reading (see Chapter 5).
- Break up texts into chunks, reading small amounts and then asking them about it.
- Practise the skill of comprehension, going back over text to look for key facts such as characters, places and so on (make it a game!).
- Teach strategies such as highlighting and underlining information in texts (see Chapter 5).
- Provide sentence starters (suggestions of how to write the beginning of a sentence) and writing frames (how to set out the written information) to help with the written part of comprehension.

Left-handedness

Some parts of writing that a right-handed person may take for granted can be tricky for left-handed children. This may include difficulties making 'finger spaces', smudging the ink/pencil of their own writing as their hand goes over what they have written, knocking their elbows into the person sat next to them (if they are right-handed) and struggling to write neatly.

How can we help?

- If the child is writing in pen, use pens which don't have 'wet' ink as they are less likely to smudge. If they are writing in pencil, look at the softness of the pencil type and try ones that are less likely to smudge.
- Help children with their pencil grip, if needed.
- If at school, think about who they are sat next to and the spacing between the children to ensure they can write comfortably without colliding elbows.
- Re-think 'pen licences' at school (a reward for being able to write neatly enough to now use a pen instead of a pencil).
- When writing, encourage children to try turning the paper, pointing the bottom right corner towards them to see if this helps.
- Provide extra handwriting support if needed.
- Try writing slopes – these are slopes for children to place their paper on in order to write. In my experience, they can be helpful for some left-handed children.

Motor skill difficulties

In my first book, *100 Ways Your Child Can Learn Through Play*, there was a big focus on motor skills development in many of the activities listed. In this book, I've tried to include as many reading and writing activities as I can that also help develop motor skills, the reason being that motor skill difficulties can be a big barrier to writing. Motor skills are split into gross and fine motor. Gross motor skills are those that use the big muscles – we use them to jump, climb and so on, but we also need them for postural control and to be able to sit comfortably to write. Fine motor skill activities are those that develop the tiny muscles in our fingers and hands, needed to be able to hold a pencil and write, zip up a coat or do up a button. Some children with specific SEND and or those who are struggling to write comfortably may need additional time on these skills.

How can we help?

- If a child has SEND and has advice from an occupational therapist (OT), implement their suggestions and strategies to help.
- Use play-based fine motor skills activities that are age appropriate (i.e., not too 'babyish' for older children) to help practise these skills regularly. You will find them scattered throughout this book in Chapters 1, 2, 3 and 4 and in my first book.

How to use this book

The first four chapters of the book focus on activity ideas, split into Sensory Ways, Imaginative Play Ways, Crafty Ways and Active Ways. Dip in and out of the activities, adapt them to suit the children in your care and have fun. Parents in particular, remember you are the experts of your own children — if the activity isn't quite suited to your child, mix it up and make it so it works. The final chapter contains my 'hacks' for reading and writing in everyday life, some of which will, I hope, address (and suggest solutions to) the key barriers to children's success and love of reading and writing. These 'hacks' don't claim to be 'ground-breaking' suggestions, but simple strategies that you can incorporate into everyday life.

Here's what you can expect in each chapter:

Chapter 1: Sensory Ways
This chapter focuses on incorporating children's senses into their literacy play. Many of the activities here involve reading and writing individual words, which is useful for all ages and abilities, building confidence with and learning spellings and tricky words and reinforcing correct letter formation. Don't skip this chapter just because the children in your care can read and write sentences; I believe it is still very important to revisit key words. The activities in this chapter might make a fun way of practising weekly spellings, for example.

These activities are a good advert for words being fun (which is often half the battle!). You'll find a real, varied and unique selection of activities listed here – I hope there is something for everyone.

I chose sensory play as it stimulates a child's senses and for many children is a wonderful way to learn. Using a multi-sensory approach (where many senses are used in one activity, such as sight, sound, smell) can be particularly helpful for children with dyslexia, helping them to remember and learn words and spellings more easily.

For some children with SEND, sensory play can be incredibly therapeutic too. It can be calming after a difficult day or be a 'go-to' activity when they are feeling overstimulated.

Chapter 2: Imaginative Play Ways

In this chapter, I share with you some fun, engaging, make-believe play activities that have reading and writing subtly woven into them. These are brilliant for embracing play and children's interests, while also enabling opportunities for writing sentences and practising extended writing. As with all the activities, they are suitable for in school or at home. The trick with these activities is to do them so that the children do not even realize you're trying to improve their reading and writing in the process. My biggest piece of advice for imaginative play activities is to throw yourself into them too! Have fun and share the giggles. This chapter has a whole range of activities, from pretend trips to the opticians to pet shows and letters in a bottle. Feel free to tweak them to fit with the child's interests and hobbies.

Chapter 3: Crafty Ways

Here I have incorporated reading and writing into crafts. Arts and crafts can be really enjoyable for some children. Colouring, drawing, cutting, sticking and creating are also fantastic for developing a whole range of other skills too, such as motor skills, concentration and problem-solving. The crafts chosen in this chapter are all easy to resource, so there's no need to go out and buy lots of craft materials.

Chapter 4: Active Ways

Some children find sitting still to read and write really challenging, for various different reasons. It may be that they simply *need* to be up and about moving around. Therefore, I've written this chapter in order to embrace this! Instead of trying to stop them from running, jumping, climbing and playing, I'm asking you instead to join them and just subtly bring some reading and writing activities along with you. Getting children to move around while learning also has the added bonus of actually helping them find sitting at a table to write later on *easier*. This is because all these big movements of jumping, climbing and running in fact help to develop the gross motor skills that they need to be able to sit comfortably and write.

Chapter 5: Everyday Hacks

Here you'll find lots of 'hacks' – hints and tips for how to make reading and writing easier for the children that you are parenting or teaching, from ways to embrace the technology available to how to make reading and writing just a 'normal' part of everyday life. This chapter reflects on some of the barriers to reading and writing explained in the Introduction and looks to suggest suitable, tangible solutions to make reading and writing easier for children.

Throughout the book I refer to a collection of skills that the activities may also help to develop alongside their reading and writing skills. These are explained below:

Language and communication: Activities that tick this box will be the ones that help children to practise either verbal communication or communication through sign language or visuals. Developing language and communication skills can also help children with their reading and writing.

Numeracy: Activities that tick this box are those that develop children's maths skills.

Concentration: Any of the activities that require your child to focus for a period of time will help to develop this skill. Concentration is also an important skill for reading and writing for periods of time.

Social skills: These are the skills that are needed in social situations. Examples include taking turns, learning to lose or win gracefully and working as a team.

Problem-solving: Activities that will tick this box will be those that require children to analyse a situation and find a solution themselves.

Motor skills: These include fine and gross motor skills, which are both needed in order to be able to write with a pen or pencil and are therefore very important to continue to develop before and alongside literacy skills.

Emotional regulation: This is the skill of managing their own emotions. This could be learning ways that help them feel calm when they are feeling overstimulated.

Sensory integration: Activities that tick this box require children to learn to process and organize sensory information (touch, sight, sounds, smells, taste, body position and movement) to carry out an activity.

Working memory: These activities require children to remember information, perhaps in an order, for a short amount of time in order to successfully carry out the task. In terms of literacy, these skills may be particularly useful when a child is completing a comprehension task or organizing their ideas to carry out some written work.

CHAPTER 1

SENSORY WAYS

1. WORD WATER BALLOON POP

Description

Write, read, pop and splash! This silly and fun activity will not only help children to practise their writing and reading skills but also provide a lot of laughs!

Equipment

Balloons, water, outdoor space, protective sheet and a marker pen.

How to

1. Together with the children, in an outdoor space, fill up a few balloons with water (even better if you have water balloons). Tie the ends of the balloons.
2. Ask the children to write some key words on the balloons (these could be ones they are practising to read/spell at the moment).
3. Line the balloons up in an outdoor space. Shout out one of the words on the balloons and ask a child to pop the correct balloon!

Alternatives

You could do this indoors by simply blowing the balloons up with air and asking the children to pop the correct ones.

Extras

Why not use food colouring to fill the balloons with different coloured water? Use a protective sheet if you do use food colouring.

Tips

Take your time setting up; the activity isn't just about popping the balloons but the whole process, from writing and reading them to popping them at the end.

SKILLS

☐ Language & communication	☐ Social skills	☐ Emotional regulation
☐ Numeracy	☑ Problem-solving	☑ Sensory integration
☑ Concentration	☑ Motor skills	☑ Working memory

2. BLOW PAINT WORDS

Description
This activity definitely has the 'wow factor'...and while it may seem a lot of effort for learning how to read or spell one word, I can assure you this activity will stick with them for a long time! It's also a lot of fun.

Equipment
Poster paints, straws, paper and a pen.

How to
1. Write down with the children a key word or spelling they are working on at the moment as big as you can on an A4 piece of paper.
2. Encourage the children to put a blob of paint at the start of each letter of the word.
3. With their straws they now need to blow the paint in the direction of the shape of the letters drawn.
4. Their aim is to write the word with the blown paint.

Alternatives
Instead of blowing the paint, you could place a blob of paint at the start of each letter and encourage the children to drag the paint along the lines of the letters using a cocktail stick. This has the added bonus of helping to develop fine motor skills in the process.

Extras
Use their blow paint key words as a display to help them remember these words.

Tips
Be sure to risk assess this, making sure that the children taking part won't accidentally ingest the paint.

SKILLS

☐ Language & communication	☐ Social skills	☐ Emotional regulation
☐ Numeracy	☑ Problem-solving	☐ Sensory integration
☑ Concentration	☑ Motor skills	☐ Working memory

3. NATURE COLLAGE WORDS

Description
This lovely multi-sensory activity is a great, stealthy way of learning key words! Children will enjoy collecting various natural objects to use to form their words.

Equipment
Bags, glue and paper.

How to
1. Either in an outdoor space or on a walk, encourage the children to collect (safe) natural objects such as sticks, pebbles, leaves and pine cones and put them in a bag.
2. Once these are collected, ask the children to write down one of the key words they are focusing on, as big as they can, on a piece of paper.
3. Support them in gluing their natural objects on the letters to form their key words.

Alternatives
If you're lucky enough to live near the beach, making the key words out of shells and sand would look brilliant. Or if you have no outdoor space access, why not use plastic building blocks?

Extras
Once their words have dried, encourage the children to close their eyes and trace their finger over the shape of the letters, saying each letter out loud as they go.

Tips
The natural objects need to be dry to stick onto the paper. It may be worth splitting this activity in two, to allow time for them to dry sufficiently.

SKILLS
☑ Language & communication	☐ Social skills	☐ Emotional regulation
☐ Numeracy	☐ Problem-solving	☑ Sensory integration
☑ Concentration	☑ Motor skills	☐ Working memory

4. SENSORY PAINT BAG WORDS

Description

Help children to create their very own sensory paint bags to practise writing and spelling words with their fingers. The beauty of this activity is that if they make a mistake they simple squish the bag and the error disappears! These make an interesting alternative to mini whiteboards in a classroom too.

Equipment

Zip-lock bags, poster paint and tape.

How to

1. Encourage the children to choose their favourite paint colour and squirt it into a zip-lock bag. Close the bag and secure using tape.
2. Tell them a key word, let them have a go at writing it on their paint bag with their fingers.
3. Reset the bags by squishing the paint and try again with a new word.

Alternatives

Instead of the children hearing a word and then writing it, you could write down the key words for them to copy. Put these either in front of them or even underneath their paint bag.

Extras

Add glitter, sequins or more than one colour of paint to make the bags even more exciting.

Tips

The bigger the zip-lock bags the better. If you don't have these, you can use any transparent plastic bags, as long as you ensure the openings are sealed securely. Take care to not overfill the bags.

SKILLS

☑ Language & communication	☐ Social skills	☐ Emotional regulation
☐ Numeracy	☑ Problem-solving	☑ Sensory integration
☑ Concentration	☑ Motor skills	☐ Working memory

5. ICE WRITING

Description

If children are lacking motivation to put pen to paper, swap the paper for some ice and the pen for a paintbrush! While they may not have space to write pieces of extended writing on their sheet of ice, they can use it as a fun way to practise writing key words and spellings.

Equipment

Oven dish, tray, water, freezer, paintbrushes and paints.

How to

1. Fill an oven dish with water. Leave it in the freezer overnight.
2. Tip out the sheet of ice onto a tray. Set the children up with paints and paintbrushes.
3. Encourage the children to practise writing words on the ice with their paintbrush.

Alternatives

Freeze water in an ice cube tray instead and ask the children to paint individual letters on each cube. They can then rearrange the cubes on the tray to make key words. You could even make an anagram for them to solve!

Extras

If you have a transparent tray, try writing key words on a piece of paper, put it underneath the tray and encourage the children to have a go at tracing the letters from a tricky word onto the ice.

Tips

To help get the ice sheet out of the tray easily, try lining the tray with clingfilm or foil.

SKILLS

- ☐ Language & communication
- ☐ Numeracy
- ☑ Concentration
- ☐ Social skills
- ☑ Problem-solving
- ☑ Motor skills
- ☐ Emotional regulation
- ☑ Sensory integration
- ☐ Working memory

6. CLINGFILM EASEL WRITING

Description

Writing on a vertical surface with the light shining through is not only a lovely sensory experience but fantastic for gross motor skills. So, make your very own transparent easel by attaching clingfilm across the bottom of two chair legs.

Equipment

Clingfilm, chair and dry erase pens.

How to

1. Wrap the clingfilm between two legs of a chair to create a transparent, vertical writing surface.
2. Give children some key words or short sentences to have a go at writing on their clingfilm.
3. If there is more than one child trying this activity, encourage them to swap places and read each other's writing.

Alternatives

If you have a tuff tray with legs or a small coffee table, you could turn it upside down and attach the clingfilm between two legs instead.

Extras

Incorporate this into other activities, for example spelling practice and story writing.

Tips

Ensure the chairs are stable enough to not fall over.

SKILLS

☐ Language & communication   ☐ Social skills   ☐ Emotional regulation
☐ Numeracy   ☑ Problem-solving   ☑ Sensory integration
☑ Concentration   ☑ Motor skills   ☐ Working memory

7. STRING THE SENTENCE

Description

Together with the children, have a go at making sentences by forming the letters of the words out of string. This is a memorable activity for reinforcing letter formation and giving children more time to remember the spellings of a word.

Equipment

String, PVA glue and card.

How to

1. Support the children in reading out loud key words or sentences and then shaping their string to make these words.
2. Stick them down onto the card using PVA glue and leave to dry.
3. Once dry, encourage the children to close their eyes and feel the string words and 'read' what they can feel.

Alternatives

String is great for cursive or joined-up writing. You can use cooked spaghetti or pipe-cleaners instead to form the letters.

Extras

Paint the string words using poster paints and display them to help children remember key spellings/words.

Tips

It may be easier for the children to write the words first in pencil and then stick the string onto the words.

SKILLS

☑ Language & communication	☐ Social skills	☐ Emotional regulation
☐ Numeracy	☐ Problem-solving	☑ Sensory integration
☑ Concentration	☑ Motor skills	☐ Working memory

8. RAINBOW CHOCOLATE TRAY

Description
Perhaps the best-smelling, most colourful writing activity you'll come across! The yummy whiff of chocolate is more than enough to encourage even the most reluctant writers to come and have a go.

Equipment
Paper, felt tips, tray and cocoa powder.*

How to
1. Encourage the children to colour a piece of paper in with a rainbow pattern.
2. Put the piece of paper at the bottom of a tray and cover with cocoa powder.
3. Write a key word on a separate piece of paper for the children. Ask them to copy it in their tray using just their finger to expose the rainbow colours under the cocoa powder.
4. Shake the tray to erase and start again.

Alternatives
Instead of cocoa powder you can use cous cous, sand, sugar and so on. Children can also use a paintbrush instead of their finger if preferred.

Extras
Incorporate this into other activities, for example spelling practice and story writing.

Tips
*Ensure to check for any relevant allergens.

SKILLS

☐ Language & communication	☐ Social skills	☐ Emotional regulation
☐ Numeracy	☐ Problem-solving	☑ Sensory integration
☑ Concentration	☑ Motor skills	☐ Working memory

9. MUSICAL SPELLING

Description

Every time I write the word 'friends' I still spell out the letters to a song I was taught in primary school, and I'm sure I'm not the only one who still sings the alphabet song when I'm working out the alphabetical order. Attaching a letter to a note of music in a tune can be a fantastic way of learning spellings for some children.

Equipment

Music player, pencil and a pen.

How to

1. Choose a simple, well-known tune (nursery rhymes are great) and a spelling they are learning.
2. Support the children in writing the spelling down and counting the sounds in the word.
3. Sing together the letters of the word to the tune.
4. Repeat.

Alternatives

If you have a keyboard or other musical instrument use this instead of a music player.

Extras

Record it so that you can play it back.

Tips

It's all about a catchy tune and repetition!

SKILLS

☑ Language & communication   ☐ Social skills   ☐ Emotional regulation
☑ Numeracy   ☐ Problem-solving   ☑ Sensory integration
☑ Concentration   ☐ Motor skills   ☐ Working memory

10. QUILL WRITING

Description
If you're looking for a unique way to encourage some writing, why not make a quill together? Thanks to various popular films and books, all things historical and magical have become popular with kids.

Equipment
Wooden skewers or straws, paper, PVA glue, poster paint and paper.

How to
1. If like me, you've no quills to hand (!) encourage your children to make their own using a wooden skewer or a straw. Simply cut out two 2cm-wide strips of paper and cut regular snips into one side of each one making them frilled like the barbs of a feather. Stick with PVA glue to the top half of skewer and leave to dry.
2. Encourage the children to dip the end of their 'quill' into some paint.
3. They can then use their quills to write with. Perhaps they could write a historical letter or a diary entry.

Alternatives
Go for a nature hunt to find some real feathers (and give them a quick clean before you use them).

Extras
Decant the paint into a pot that looks like an ink pot used for quills.

Tips
The children will need to dip their quill into the paint very regularly. Risk assess if you use wooden skewers.

SKILLS

☐ Language & communication	☐ Social skills	☐ Emotional regulation
☐ Numeracy	☑ Problem-solving	☑ Sensory integration
☑ Concentration	☑ Motor skills	☐ Working memory

CHAPTER 2

IMAGINATIVE PLAY WAYS

11. TOY MUSEUM

Description
Children often love showing their toys to others. Embrace this to encourage some writing by asking them to make their very own toy museum (complete with signs!). Let them take you on a tour of their various exhibits.

Equipment
Pencil, paper, sticky tape and toys.

How to
1. Discuss what the children know about museums. Ask them where they would see writing in a museum.
2. Help them to plan their very own toy museum.
3. Support them in setting it up, complete with signs and descriptions for each exhibit.
4. Allow them the opportunity to show others their museum, reading the signs and descriptions of the exhibit to their peers or adults.

Alternatives
Make a small world play museum instead, perhaps with toy dinosaurs to replicate the dinosaur exhibitions at the Natural History Museum!

Extras
To encourage even more writing, children can create posters or brochures for the museum too.

Tips
Let the children choose the toys – the more passionate they are about the 'exhibitions' the more encouraged they may be to write. Provide key words mats if needed (see Chapter 5).

SKILLS

☑ Language & communication	☑ Social skills	☐ Emotional regulation
☐ Numeracy	☑ Problem-solving	☐ Sensory integration
☐ Concentration	☐ Motor skills	☐ Working memory

12. SPY LETTERS

Description
While pretending to be spies, children can enjoy writing secret, invisible messages to one another that only show up after being painted!

Equipment
Water colour paints, paintbrushes, white wax crayons, water and paper.

How to
1. Help the children to pretend to be spies. Ask them to write a secret message on a piece of white paper with their white wax crayon.
2. Swap messages and paint over them with water colour paints and read.
3. Repeat.

Alternatives
Pretend the children are the police and write an important 'clue' for a crime on a piece of paper with a white wax crayon for them to decipher and read.

Extras
Add extra props to help children get into character. These could be items such as magnifying glasses, hats, sunglasses and lab coats!

Tips
Give children examples of messages before they start and some sentence starters, if needed. A blank piece of paper can often be very daunting (see Chapter 5 for tips).

SKILLS

☑ Language & communication	☑ Social skills	☐ Emotional regulation
☐ Numeracy	☑ Problem-solving	☐ Sensory integration
☐ Concentration	☑ Motor skills	☐ Working memory

13. PET SHOW

Description

Roll up, roll up for the toy pet show! A PURRfect opportunity to practise those writing skills when scoring each animal in their CATegory.

Equipment

Toy animals, pens, paper and clipboards (optional extra).

How to

1. Gather some toy animals together and encourage the children to set up a pet show!
2. Discuss what you will be scoring the animals on, for example 'softness' or their tricks.
3. Ask the children to write down their scoring criteria in a list. This is a great exercise for thinking about adjectives.
4. Give them time to walk around and look at the various animals, giving them a score out of ten for each criterion.

Alternatives

Instead of a pet show, you could do a biscuit/cake contest (taking into consideration any allergies). Children can try the different treats and score them on criteria such as 'sweetness'.

Extras

Why not go the 'whole hog' and create tickets and posters as well as certificates and medals for the winning animals?

Tips

In order for the children to know what to expect, show them photographs or videos of a pet competition.

SKILLS

☑ Language & communication	☑ Social skills	☐ Emotional regulation
☑ Numeracy	☐ Problem-solving	☐ Sensory integration
☐ Concentration	☐ Motor skills	☐ Working memory

14. DRIVING DOWN MASKING TAPE BOULEVARD

Description
This is perhaps the sneakiest way to get some reading and writing into children's play. Children will love creating a network of roads with masking tape on the floor to drive toy cars down – it just needs someone to write the street names!

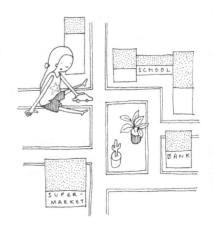

Equipment
Pencils, toy cars, paper, masking tape, cardboard boxes and a hard floor.*

How to
1. Provide the children with masking tape and toy cars. Help them to stick the tape to the floor to create a network of roads for their cars.
2. For each 'road', ask them to write a road sign on paper to stick down.
3. Get them to position the cardboard boxes on the streets as buildings and ask them to write the names of the buildings on them. For example, 'police station'.
4. Let them play with the set-up.

Alternatives
Instead of masking tape, use chalk outside.

Extras
Ask children how to get to certain buildings from a starting point. Ask them to write down the directions.

Tips
*Make sure that the tape won't damage the floor you've chosen.

SKILLS

☑ Language & communication ☑ Social skills ☐ Emotional regulation
☐ Numeracy ☑ Problem-solving ☐ Sensory integration
☐ Concentration ☑ Motor skills ☑ Working memory

15. WANTED TEDDY POSTER

Description
Create the scene of a teddy escaping from soft-toy prison! It is the children's job to create a 'wanted poster' to put up to help find the teddy.

Equipment
Camera, printer, paper, glue stick and scissors.

How to
1. Tell the children all about the teddy that has escaped from toy prison. Explain that they need to create a 'wanted poster' to put up.
2. Discuss the structure of the poster, the picture, the sentence to explain what has happened and the money for the reward.
3. Give the children time to write their posters then put them up.
4. Continue the story by someone 'telephoning' you to say they have found the teddy!

Alternatives
Instead, it can be a lost teddy and the children have to create missing posters for it.

Extras
Take photographs of the teddy (up to no good) beforehand that the children can use for their posters.

Tips
Don't presume children will know what a wanted poster is. Show them some examples and provide key words and structure if needed (see Chapter 5 for tips).

SKILLS

☑ Language & communication	☑ Social skills	☐ Emotional regulation
☑ Numeracy	☑ Problem-solving	☐ Sensory integration
☐ Concentration	☑ Motor skills	☐ Working memory

16. WORD FISHING

Description
Using a pencil, some sticky tack, paper and a sprinkle of imagination, transform your room into a fishing lake to do some serious word angling!

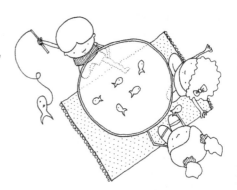

Equipment
Paper, pencils, thread, scissors, sticky tack and a tray.

How to
1. Support the children to cut out ten pieces of paper to make fishes.
2. Write a word that they are learning to read or spell onto each fish.
3. Make the fishing rods by sticking some sticky tack onto the end of a pencil.
4. Read out one of the words, ask the children to find it and 'fish it' by pressing their 'fishing rod' onto the paper fish.

Alternatives
Attach thread to the pencil, put a magnet on the end of the string and connect paper fasteners to the fish. This would make a more realistic fishing rod that picks up the fish using a magnetic force.

Extras
Hold a competition to see who can fish the word out the quickest after you have read it.

Tips
Let the children practise with their fishing rods first to make sure they can pick up the fish, before you read the words out.

SKILLS

☐ Language & communication   ☐ Social skills   ☐ Emotional regulation
☑ Numeracy   ☑ Problem-solving   ☐ Sensory integration
☑ Concentration   ☑ Motor skills   ☑ Working memory

17. LET'S GO TO THE OPTICIANS

Description

Children are likely to have role-played doctors and vets...but have they played opticians yet? What's particularly wonderful about this imaginative play activity is the amount of reading and writing that's involved in their play.

Equipment

Pencils, paper, sticky tack and a clipboard (optional extra).

How to

1. Talk about the opticians, what happens there and why.
2. Encourage the children to set up the role-play activity. This involves creating a chart of letters to go on the wall that they need to read. The letters need to be in lines, with the letters decreasing in size the further down the paper they read.
3. Children also need to create a patient form. This can have questions such as name, age, which line they were able to read, if they need glasses and so on.
4. Let the children enjoy taking it in turns to play at being the optician, asking their patient to sit on a chair and read from the chart, filling in the form as they go.

Alternatives

Why not play dentists instead? This can create writing opportunities when the 'dentist' fills in the patient form.

Extras

Stretch the children's writing and reading by asking them to make the patient questionnaire even more detailed. They could include the patient's address, for example.

Tips

Don't presume children will know what happens at the opticians.

SKILLS

☑ Language & communication	☑ Social skills	☐ Emotional regulation
☑ Numeracy	☐ Problem-solving	☐ Sensory integration
☐ Concentration	☐ Motor skills	☐ Working memory

18. WITCH'S POTION RECIPE

Description
Reading the recipe carefully, with a sprinkle of mud, a spoonful of leaves and a dash of pebbles, you can create a magical potion together!

Equipment
Plastic containers, soil, water, pebbles, twigs, leaves and pine cones (optional extras).

How to
1. Present the children with their very own Witch's Potion Recipe! To make this just write a list of various ingredients (with amounts) on a piece of paper. For example, 3 tablespoons of soil, 1 cup of water.
2. Provide the children with containers and access to the ingredients. Ask them to read and follow the recipe to create the potion.
3. Once completed, ask them to write a recipe for someone else.

Alternatives
Try this inside with ingredients such as cocoa powder, sugar, water and glitter.

Extras
Children could pour the potions into jam jars and write labels for each potion.

Tips
Make the potion recipe look more realistic by writing it with fancy handwriting on brown paper and tearing the edges. Risk assess, to ensure children won't ingest the potions.

SKILLS

☑ Language & communication	☑ Social skills	☐ Emotional regulation
☑ Numeracy	☑ Problem-solving	☐ Sensory integration
☐ Concentration	☐ Motor skills	☐ Working memory

19. SALT DOUGH SENTENCE ARCHAEOLOGY PART 1 – WRITING

Description

Have fun creating pretend ancient secrets together with this science-based activity. Use salt dough to form the pretend archaeological findings complete with writing, ready to be discovered. It is much easier than it sounds, and a lovely way to practise writing using a different medium.

Equipment

3/4 cup water, 1 cup table salt, 2 cups flour, bowl, mixing spoon, pencil and a tray.

How to

1. Mix the water, salt and flour together in a bowl. Take out of the bowl, place on a floured surface and knead.
2. Split the dough into several hand-sized balls, one for each child. Ask the children to flatten their salt dough to make a long rectangular piece and write a sentence into it, using an old pencil.
3. Leave to dry, either air drying overnight or in an oven for an hour or so at a very low temperature (checking regularly until hard).

Alternatives

Make more temporary versions using play dough.

Extras

Once dry, children can paint them to make them more realistic.

Tips

Save their archaeological sentences for part 2.

SKILLS

☐ Language & communication	☐ Social skills	☐ Emotional regulation
☑ Numeracy	☑ Problem-solving	☑ Sensory integration
☑ Concentration	☑ Motor skills	☐ Working memory

20. SALT DOUGH SENTENCE ARCHAEOLOGY PART 2 - READING

Description
Transport the children into the wonderful world of archaeology! Their job now is to carefully uncover the various salt dough sentences (created in part 1) and have a go at reading them.

Equipment
Salt dough sentences made in part 1, cous cous, trays and paintbrushes.

How to
1. Lay the salt dough sentences on a tray and cover with cous cous (this is the dirt at the archaeological dig site!).
2. Encourage children to carefully use their paintbrushes to uncover the salt dough sentences.
3. Once they've found one, ask them to have a go at reading it.

Alternatives
Take this activity outside and place the words in a sandpit or under some soil.

Extras
Children can have a go at creating 'rubbings' of the sentences by placing a piece of paper over the top of the sentence and gently rubbing the paper with a pencil.

Tips
Make sure to do part 1 first!

SKILLS

☑ Language & communication	☐ Social skills	☐ Emotional regulation
☐ Numeracy	☑ Problem-solving	☑ Sensory integration
☑ Concentration	☑ Motor skills	☐ Working memory

21. LET'S BE PHOTOGRAPHERS

Description
Try taking some photographs together with the children, printing them and writing underneath each photo. Caption writing can be great for encouraging putting pen to paper as captions are short and snappy by nature.

Equipment
Camera, printer, paper, glue stick and scissors.

How to
1. While out and about take some photographs. These could be to document a walk or specific things in an outdoor space, such as birds.
2. Print off the photographs and support the children in cutting and sticking them onto paper or a notebook.
3. Ask them to write a sentence underneath each photo to explain what it shows.

Alternatives
Instead of printing the photographs, help them practise their typing skills by creating a photo scrap book on the computer (see Chapter 5 for more technology tips).

Extras
Swap their photographs and captions with others to read.

Tips
Provide example captions, writing frames and key words to support.

SKILLS

☑ Language & communication	☐ Social skills	☐ Emotional regulation
☐ Numeracy	☐ Problem-solving	☐ Sensory integration
☑ Concentration	☐ Motor skills	☑ Working memory

CHAPTER 3

CRAFTY WAYS

22. PAPER CHAIN SENTENCES

Description
Sentences don't just have to be created with a pen or pencil on some lined paper! Why not build sentences by physically connecting words together in a paper chain? It's still the same task, but with a sprinkle of creativity and enjoyment.

Equipment
Coloured paper, scissors, glue sticks and pens.

How to
1. Ask the children to cut out a few 5cm-wide strips of paper.
2. Decide on sentence ideas. It could be for a display in their room/classroom 'Welcome to...' or a sentence about a book you're reading. Ask them to write the words from the sentence they've chosen on each strip of paper.
3. Encourage them to connect the words together to make a paper chain! They need to glue the ends of the first strip together so that it makes a ring. They then put the next strip through the centre of the ring before connecting them together, and so on with the rest of the strips.

Alternatives
Use this activity to introduce connectives (words that join sentences together) such as 'and' and 'because'. Children can make two parts of a sentence first and then choose a special 'connective' strip of paper to join them together.

Extras
Help the children to improve their sentences by providing them with adjectives or adverbs on strips of paper that they can add in.

Tips
When the children are sticking the strips to make the chain, help them to check that the words are on the outside.

SKILLS

☑ Language & communication	☐ Social skills	☐ Emotional regulation
☑ Numeracy	☑ Problem-solving	☐ Sensory integration
☐ Concentration	☑ Motor skills	☐ Working memory

23. LETTER IN A BOTTLE

Description

I still remember as a child actually finding a letter in a bottle on a beach in Spain and it being one of the most exciting moments of my childhood! Recreate this together to encourage some lovely reading and writing.

Equipment

Paper, empty glass bottle, pencil, ribbon and a cork (optional extra) for each child.

How to

1. Set the scene that the children are stuck on a desert island and their only way of getting help is by sending a letter in a bottle!
2. Support them in writing the letter, show them examples and give them the structure.
3. Once they've written it, ask them to roll it then secure it with a ribbon and place it inside the glass bottle.
4. Swap bottles to read someone else's letter.

Alternatives

Focus on reading instead by creating the letter in the bottle in advance for children to find and read.

Extras

Make the letter look old and more realistic by tearing the edges of the paper and colouring it brown using coffee or tea bags.

Tips

Give them sentence starters to support (see the writing tips in Chapter 5).

SKILLS

- ☑ Language & communication
- ☐ Numeracy
- ☐ Concentration
- ☑ Social skills
- ☑ Problem-solving
- ☑ Motor skills
- ☐ Emotional regulation
- ☐ Sensory integration
- ☐ Working memory

24. SPELLING WANDS

Description
Are there some words that the children are just finding too tricky to spell at the moment? No worries, use some 'magic' to help turn their pencils into spelling wands with this enchanted craft activity!

Equipment
Pencils, yellow card, pens, sticky tape, colouring pens and sequins (optional extra).

How to
1. Ask children to cut out a large star shape from some yellow card.
2. On each point of the star, they need to write a word they are finding hard to spell.
3. Provide them with colouring pens and sequins to decorate their star.
4. Secure the star to the end of the pencil with sticky tape.

Alternatives
Use sticks found outside instead of their pencils.

Extras
Make spelling wands for certain spelling groups, for example words beginning with 'th'.

Tips
Star shapes are tricky to draw, so provide a template for the children if necessary.

SKILLS

☐ Language & communication	☐ Social skills	☐ Emotional regulation
☑ Numeracy	☑ Problem-solving	☐ Sensory integration
☑ Concentration	☐ Motor skills	☑ Working memory

25. TAPE ART GRAFFITI

Description

Perhaps the coolest way to practise spelling and reading words is to make them with this tape art graffiti craft! This quick and easy craft is fantastic for engaging children in literacy while enabling them to perfect their creativity.

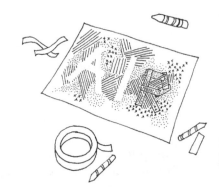

Equipment

Paper, masking tape, coloured crayons or paints and brushes.

How to

1. Choose a word or sentence for them to create.
2. Ask the children to make the words by sticking masking tape in the shapes of the letters onto the paper.
3. Encourage them to paint or colour on the sheet of paper over and around the masking tape to cover the whole sheet.
4. Peel off the tape to reveal the words.

Alternatives

Create outside on the ground using chalks.

Extras

You could use fabric pens and create t-shirts using this effect.

Tips

If you use paint, make sure to leave it to dry before peeling off the tape.

SKILLS

- ☐ Language & communication
- ☐ Numeracy
- ☐ Concentration
- ☐ Social skills
- ☑ Problem-solving
- ☑ Motor skills
- ☐ Emotional regulation
- ☐ Sensory integration
- ☐ Working memory

26. SENTENCE STICKS

Description
Maybe it's the colours, the use of lollipop sticks or the element of surprise...either way this crafty way of encouraging writing is a real hit with lots of kids.

Equipment
Coloured lollipop sticks, glue, paper, pens and pencils.

How to
1. In advance, write some phrases (that could be used to create a story) on small strips of paper and stick each of them on a lollipop stick. Make a handful of sticks for each of these groups: 'where' (e.g. on a beach'), 'who' (e.g. the giant) and 'what' (e.g. ran away).
2. Ask the children to choose three sentence sticks, one from each group.
3. Let them have fun writing down their stories based on the sticks they collected.

Alternatives
If you don't have lollipop sticks you can just use coloured card.

Extras
The children can help write the phrases for the lollipop sticks.

Tips
It may be useful to have different colours for each group of phrases, for example blue for 'where'.

SKILLS

☑ Language & communication ☐ Social skills ☐ Emotional regulation
☐ Numeracy ☑ Problem-solving ☐ Sensory integration
☐ Concentration ☐ Motor skills ☐ Working memory

27. MARVELLOUS MACARONI MONSTERS

Description
Write, swap and read instructions to make marvellous macaroni monsters. The silliest and scariest writing activity around!

Equipment
Paper, pencils, uncooked pasta shapes (please note these pose a choking hazard) and PVA glue.

How to
1. Give children paper to write their instructions for a macaroni monster. It needs to include: number of eyes, long/short hair, number of arms, number of legs and if they are happy/sad/angry.
2. Ask them to swap their instructions with someone else.*
3. Support them in reading the instructions and sticking the pasta to the paper to create the monster!

Alternatives
Instead of pasta, you can use craft materials or sticks and small pebbles from outside.

Extras
Encourage children to specify colours in their instructions and paint the pasta.

Tips
*If you are doing this with one child, write some instructions yourself to swap with them.

SKILLS

☑ Language & communication	☐ Social skills	☐ Emotional regulation
☑ Numeracy	☑ Problem-solving	☑ Sensory integration
☐ Concentration	☑ Motor skills	☐ Working memory

28. PET PASSPORTS

Description

Create the cutest of pretend passports, complete with photograph and information ready to send your pets on an imaginative holiday of their dreams.

Equipment

Paper, pencil, camera/camera phone, printer and a glue stick.

How to

1. Look at some photographs (or real) examples of passports and pet passports together. Set them the task of taking a photograph of their pet.
2. Fold an A4 piece of paper in half to make the passport. Ask them to create the front cover and then the page for their pet. It should include the pet's name, species, breed, gender, date of birth and colour.
3. Print off the photo of the pet to stick at the top of the passport page.

Alternatives

Create a teddy passport instead.

Extras

Play at airports, encouraging the children to read each other's passports.

Tips

Give them sentence starters or a template layout for support (see Chapter 5 for advice).

SKILLS

☑ Language & communication	☑ Social skills	☐ Emotional regulation
☐ Numeracy	☐ Problem-solving	☐ Sensory integration
☐ Concentration	☐ Motor skills	☐ Working memory

29. CARDBOARD COMPUTER

Description
That box sitting in the corridor is screaming out to be made into the most eco-friendly of computers...the cardboard computer! This is a fantastic way to get children to practise spelling and typing – with no pressure.

Equipment
Cardboard boxes, scissors, sticking tape, marker pen, paper and a pen.

How to
1. Help children to design and create a computer complete with keyboard using a cardboard box! Use a flat piece of cardboard for the keyboard and copy the letters from a real keyboard onto it in order.
2. Stick their practice spellings onto the 'screen' of their 'computer'.
3. Ask the children to copy the letters off the screen and 'type' them using the keyboard.
4. Repeat with the next word.

Alternatives
Create a tablet device instead.

Extras
Encourage them to see how fast they can type the words!

Tips
Keyboard skills are really important to learn, so make sure the pretend keyboards letters are in the correct place and order to make the practice more valuable.

SKILLS

☐ Language & communication	☐ Social skills	☐ Emotional regulation
☐ Numeracy	☑ Problem-solving	☐ Sensory integration
☑ Concentration	☑ Motor skills	☐ Working memory

CHAPTER 4

ACTIVE WAYS

30. HOOPLA

Description
Read, aim and throw! Make reading key words much more fun with this hoopla reading game. This is an enjoyable way of practising hand–eye coordination and gross motor skills too.

Equipment
Paper plates, scissors, plastic cups, paper and sticking tape.

How to
1. Children can make their hoopla hoop by cutting out the centre of a paper plate with scissors. You could ask the children to decorate it too, to give them more ownership of the task.
2. Next, write down five key words that they are practising on a small piece of paper and stick each one on an upturned plastic cup.
3. Place all the cups in a line, on a ledge or table.
4. Read out one of the words and ask them to throw their hoop over the word you just read.

Alternatives
If the children love football, you can ask them to kick a football at the correct paper cup instead, as target practice.

Extras
Swap the game round to encourage writing and ask the children to write the key words and set up the game.

Tips
Make sure the throwing distance isn't too far; the objective is to practise reading not long-distance target challenges. And the last thing you want to do is disengage the children because they can't throw their hoop over the cups.

SKILLS

☑ Language & communication	☐ Social skills	☐ Emotional regulation
☐ Numeracy	☐ Problem-solving	☐ Sensory integration
☑ Concentration	☑ Motor skills	☐ Working memory

31. WALK THE ALPHABET

Description

Enjoy an 'alphabetical walk' together. Children simply look for and write down one thing they see for each letter of the alphabet! An addictive game that is great for encouraging writing through play while out and about.

Equipment

Pencils, paper and clipboards (optional extra).

How to

1. Give the children a piece of paper and pencil and ask them to write down the letters of the alphabet in order in the margin. You may choose to do this part for them if it is too difficult.
2. Explain that when they are outside, they need to try and find one object for each letter of the alphabet and write it down on their sheet next to that letter.
3. Support with clues and spellings. Give lots of praise when they find a word.

Alternatives

If the whole alphabet seems a little daunting, choose a selection of letters instead.

Extras

If they thrive on competition, set a timer so that they can try to beat their own time next time– or enable them to compete against others.

Tips

If you don't have any outside space available, try this activity indoors.

SKILLS

☑ Language & communication	☑ Social skills	☐ Emotional regulation
☐ Numeracy	☑ Problem-solving	☐ Sensory integration
☑ Concentration	☐ Motor skills	☑ Working memory

32. STICKY NOTE REACTION SPEED WALL

Description
Write, shout, read and grab! This fast-paced game not only challenges reaction speeds but provides an exciting opportunity to practise reading key words.

Equipment
Pens and sticky notes.

How to
1. Together with the children, write down some key words, one on each sticky note.
2. Stick the sticky notes onto a wall or the back of a door.
3. Challenge the children, in turns, to read and pull off each key word as quickly as they can.
4. Have a go yourself too.

Alternatives
For some children, the pressure of a race/timer for reading can be counter-productive – if this is the case, write the words on the reverse of the sticky notes. Play the reaction speed game to collect as many sticky notes as they can in a certain time and then afterwards ask them to try and read the words on the notes they have collected.

Extras
If they thrive on competition, set a timer to beat their own time next time, or get them to compete against others.

Tips
Make sure the sticky notes will not damage the surface you've chosen to stick them onto.

SKILLS

☐ Language & communication	☑ Social skills	☐ Emotional regulation
☐ Numeracy	☐ Problem-solving	☐ Sensory integration
☑ Concentration	☑ Motor skills	☐ Working memory

33. HOP THE WORD

Description
Physically jumping from one letter to another not only helps children remember the spelling of a word but also aids gross motor skill development. It's also a useful way of recapping reading individual phonic sounds and blending them together.

Equipment
Pens, paper and masking tape.

How to
1. Together with the children choose a word they are learning to spell (this might be from their class spelling list, or a word you know they are finding difficult).
2. Break the word down into letters or phonics sounds and write each individual one on a separate piece of paper (e.g. c-h-i-p or ch-i-p).
3. Space the letters out in order and tape the paper to a hard floor.
4. Ask the children to jump from letter to letter saying each out loud as they land, before saying the entire word.

Alternatives
Use chalk outside instead.

Extras
Once they have hopped the letters, see if they can write out the key word themselves. You can also try jumbling the order of the letters up on the floor and seeing if they can jump them in order.

Tips
Make sure the tape will not damage the floor that you've chosen to stick them onto and that the paper isn't too slippery to land on.

SKILLS

☑ Language & communication	☐ Social skills	☐ Emotional regulation
☐ Numeracy	☑ Problem-solving	☐ Sensory integration
☑ Concentration	☑ Motor skills	☐ Working memory

34. CHALK WORD BASE

Description

Get your children running and reading with this very active literacy game! It's fantastic for learning to read tricky words without any pressure.

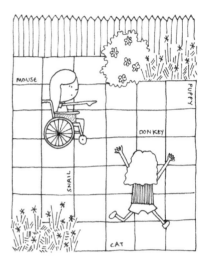

Equipment

Chalk and an outdoor space.

How to

1. With help from the children, write some key words, spaced out, on the ground outside with chalk.
2. Shout out one of the words and encourage all the children to dash to find that word and stand on it.
3. Repeat with the other words.

Alternatives

A smaller, table-top version of this game is to write the key words on a large piece of paper and encourage the child to 'splat' the word with their hand when you read it.

Extras

Swap roles with the children, encouraging them to read out the words on the ground.

Tips

Allow children time at the start to walk around and read the words beforehand. Encourage children to run to the paving slab the word is written on and not the word itself to avoid collisions.

SKILLS

☑ Language & communication	☑ Social skills	☐ Emotional regulation
☐ Numeracy	☑ Problem-solving	☐ Sensory integration
☑ Concentration	☑ Motor skills	☐ Working memory

35. WORD PONG

Description
While adults may remember a different version of this game, this activity is all about practising reading words through play. It is entertaining and very fast!

Equipment
Plastic cups, a small ball (a table tennis ball is ideal), paper and a pen.

How to
1. Set this activity up by placing a few plastic cups at each end of a desk/table (one collection of cups for each team).
2. Write words on small pieces of paper and put them in each cup.
3. If you have enough players, split into teams. Take it in turns to try and throw the ball into each other's cups. If someone gets the ball in the cup, they need to read the word found inside it before it is the next team's turn.
4. The winners are the team who have read all the words in their opponents' cups.

Alternatives
This can simply be a target practice game instead of a team game. Place the cups at one end of the table and encourage the child to throw the ball into the cups, then they need to read the word.

Extras
Encourage writing by asking the children to set the game up at the start, writing the key words for the cups.

Tips
Not all children enjoy competing against each other so you can choose to reduce the pressure by putting everyone on the same team.

SKILLS

☑ Language & communication	☑ Social skills	☐ Emotional regulation
☐ Numeracy	☑ Problem-solving	☐ Sensory integration
☑ Concentration	☑ Motor skills	☐ Working memory

36. VERB BALLS

Description
This is an exciting activity to help children learn to spell and read useful verbs (doing words). It's also wonderful for gross motor skills, aiding with accurate throwing and catching.

Equipment
Paper and a pencil.

How to
1. Discuss with the children what verbs are, and which ones you could do where you are. For example, jump, run, hop, write, sing and dance.
2. Ask one child to write a verb on a piece of paper, scrunch it up into a 'verb ball' then throw it to another child.
3. They need to open up the verb ball, read the word and act it out.
4. Repeat.

Alternatives
Do this in teams at school or with a group of children. One team writes the instructions and throws and the other team reads and acts out the verbs.

Extras
Instead of single verbs, children could be encouraged to write full sentence instructions for the action.

Tips
Provide key word prompts if needed.

SKILLS

☑ Language & communication ☑ Social skills ☐ Emotional regulation
☐ Numeracy ☑ Problem-solving ☐ Sensory integration
☑ Concentration ☑ Motor skills ☐ Working memory

37. NATURE SCAVENGER HUNT

Description

Get out into nature to encourage some writing through play. Clipboard in hand, children will have a fantastic time documenting their findings in the fresh air.

Equipment

Paper, clipboard and a pencil for each child.

How to

1. Discuss predictions of what you will see on your scavenger hunt.
2. Support the children to create a simple tick chart or tally of the things they might see on their walk.
3. Help the children to read and tick off the things they see on the walk.

Alternatives

If you don't have a clipboard, use a piece of card to rest the paper on.

Extras

On their return, ask the children to write sentences about what they found.

Tips

Ensure that children don't run with their pencil – it can be a safety risk.

SKILLS

☑ Language & communication	☑ Social skills	☐ Emotional regulation
☑ Numeracy	☐ Problem-solving	☐ Sensory integration
☑ Concentration	☑ Motor skills	☐ Working memory

38. FIND IT, WRITE IT, KEEP IT

Description
This is a really enjoyable, lively
activity that allows children to
focus on a particular letter of the
alphabet. As the title suggests,
children simply find objects, write
down their name and keep them in
the bag. Who can fill their bag first?

Equipment
Paper, pen and a bag for each child.

How to
1. Set up an area with a bag and some paper and a pen.
2. Choose a letter from the alphabet. Explain to the children that
   they need to search for as many objects as they can beginning
   with that letter.
3. Once they find an object, they need to write down its name on
   the paper and put it in the bag.
4. The winner is the person who fills their bag with the most
   objects.

Alternatives
This doesn't need to be a competition; children can just enjoy
searching for objects and filling the bag.

Extras
Strategically place objects nearby that you would like them to have
a go at spelling.

Tips
Help keep the game fun by providing support with the writing part
when needed.

SKILLS

☐ Language & communication	☑ Social skills	☐ Emotional regulation
☑ Numeracy	☑ Problem-solving	☐ Sensory integration
☐ Concentration	☐ Motor skills	☐ Working memory

39. READING WRITING RELAY

Description
Pass the baton of reading and writing with this fast-paced team game that helps children build confidence in their reading and writing skills through active play.

Equipment
Paper, pencil and kitchen roll tubes.

How to
1. Write down key words or short sentences on strips of paper and put each one inside a kitchen roll tube. Place the tubes at one end of a room/outdoor space.
2. Working in pairs, ask one child to sit at the far end away from the tubes. Encourage the other to collect a tube (baton) and run with it to their partner. They then have to open it and read the strip to them.
3. Their partner must write down on a piece of paper what they hear. They then swap roles and the writer now runs to get another tube to read to their partner.

Alternatives
This can be done without the kitchen roll tubes.

Extras
If they enjoy competition, the children could race against other pairs, or time themselves.

Tips
Let the children have a go at reading the strips informally before they start the game. They can even help write them. If you are doing this with just one child, be a part of the team together.

SKILLS

☑ Language & communication	☑ Social skills	☐ Emotional regulation
☐ Numeracy	☐ Problem-solving	☐ Sensory integration
☑ Concentration	☑ Motor skills	☐ Working memory

40. TORCH WORD SEARCH

Description
Shine a light on reading with this simple, yet unique activity. Display some key words around the room, turn off the lights and ask the children to find each one with their torch.

CAKE

Equipment
Torches, paper and a pen.

How to
1. Write key words on large pieces of paper and stick these around the room.
2. Turn off the lights, pull the curtains/blinds and turn on the torches.
3. Shout out a key word and ask the children to try and find it using their torches.
4. Repeat.

Alternatives
Stick the words onto the ceiling.

Extras
Write short sentences instead of key words for them to find.

Tips
Check for tripping hazards if children are walking around in the dark.

SKILLS

☐ Language & communication ☐ Social skills   ☑ Emotional regulation
☐ Numeracy   ☑ Problem-solving   ☑ Sensory integration
☑ Concentration   ☐ Motor skills   ☐ Working memory

CHAPTER 5

EVERYDAY HACKS

Encouraging reading and writing isn't just about activities; there are lots of other simple ways you can inspire children to pick up a book or put pen to paper. In this final chapter, I'll take you through some of my 'hacks' for home or school that may help to spark that love of literacy that is so important. It's all about simply and subtly showing children that reading and writing are useful, part of everyday life and can be enjoyable. One key point to remember with all everyday reading and writing activities is that they are achievable for the children – don't set them up to fail as you will do more harm than good. Start with the basics; we aren't just boosting their reading and writing skills but their confidence in their ability to read and write too. Many of these 'hacks' will reflect on and relate to the reading barriers discussed in the Introduction and can be done alongside the activities in the previous chapters.

READING HACKS

BE A READING ROLE MODEL

Children often look up to their families and their teachers to set the example. If we are always on a smart phone, they are likely to do the same as they grow up. But if they see us taking pleasure to sit and read a book, they too may be encouraged to do the same. So, at every opportunity possible, show them (if you can) that you enjoy reading. Let them see you sitting down reading a book. Normalize it. I can guarantee that this has a bigger impact than 'nagging' children to read their reading books.

As I mentioned in the Introduction, I am aware that reading doesn't come easily to all adults and I think it's important to recognize this and show children it can be difficult for us too. Be open when you can't read something and need to look it up. Explain when reading is frustrating for you. Let them see you seeking out extra help if you need it. They need to know that they aren't the only ones finding the English language tricky and we all make mistakes. It's how we respond to these challenges that is important.

SHOW THE SUBTITLES

In my opinion, this is the easiest way you can improve children's reading ability. It requires almost zero effort on both parts. Most televisions or streaming devices have the subtitle option. Simply go into the settings and turn on subtitles for when they watch a programme on television. You could do this at home or, if you're a teacher, in your classroom. Children are likely to get so used to having the subtitles on that they will forget they are there but, importantly, they will start to read and associate the words spoken on the screen with the words printed.

READ TO YOUR PET

. . . .

When we bought our pet hamster, Nibbles, from the pet shop last year, the sales assistant told our children that it was very important that they read to Nibbles every evening after school. My husband and I gave each other a sideways glance, thinking, did we hear this right? Is this scientifically correct? But that sales assistant, perhaps without even realizing her impact, has ensured that not only is our hamster perhaps the most 'well-read' hamster in the UK (!) but our children have been motivated to read more often. And it turns out that pets make excellent listeners. Unlike adults, they don't (unwittingly) put pressure on the reader, they don't interrupt, and they never correct. And while it is important for children to read to adults so that they can correct and support with tricky words, it's also okay to read for fun, without the stress of reading a text correctly. Let them work it out slowly and calmly in their own time. If you don't have a pet (or school pet), I'm certainly not suggesting you dash out and buy one for this purpose! Instead, think of your options for a reading audience. If you're a parent or carer, what about grandparents? What about a baby sibling? Is it less stressful to read to family over a video call? Or more fun reading to teddies? If you're a teacher, could children read to younger year groups? Parent helpers? Be guided by the children and embrace it. Their preference may change over time, but that's equally okay.

READ THE INSTRUCTIONS

If you're building a new flat-pack cabinet or trying out a new recipe for a chocolate cake, ask your children to help you read the instructions or recipe. Help them to feel that reading a simple one-line instruction is going to be hugely helpful to you, making them feel valued. The same goes for writing; if you need to suddenly jot down something to remember, ask them to do it or at least part of it. And praise and thank them when they do. This small adjustment, done regularly, can make a big impact on reading and writing skills, and confidence.

WORDS ARE ALL AROUND US

From street signs to menus, words are literally all around us. Use this to your advantage! If as a parent you are on a walk with your children, read signs to them, and ask them to read them too. In a restaurant, see if they'd like to read something off the menu. Importantly, frame it as a game or as them helping you out...not extra reading practice. At school, encourage children to read the notices, displays, any words in the playground. You'll find that over time they will start pointing out and reading words independently themselves too.

PUT THE WORDS UP

Ensure that words are on display and accessible for children to practise reading – this is almost always, in my experience, done well at schools. But key words could also be displayed at home too. Seeing and reading them regularly, in their own time, can be helpful to children in learning how to read key words and how they are spelt. It is very important to remember that too many words on display can be distracting and unlikely to help. And for some children a distracting environment can be very overstimulating. So always be led by the children's experience.

DOES IT MATTER WHAT THEY READ?

Reading should be enjoyable and hopefully become a hobby. For this to happen, I strongly believe in reading material being a choice. If the goal is to enable children to enjoy reading and be successful at it, does it matter (within reason) *what* they read? It doesn't have to be a fiction book, it could be a book about dinosaurs, farms, trains, fairies – whatever they are interested in. This could be particularly important for children who have special interests, for example some autistic children. I'd also argue it doesn't have to be a *book* (!); comics, for example, can be useful for some children with dyslexia (with the chunks of small text).

Some children need a purpose to read, so that it doesn't seem pointless to them. So, give them a purpose. It may be a toy catalogue, an instruction manual or a holiday brochure...be led by the children and what they are interested in. And, as I mentioned in the Introduction, make sure the book/text doesn't just match their reading age but their interest age too; 'babyish' books are unlikely to instill a love of reading.

BOOK BINGO

This activity can be a lovely way to encourage a breadth of reading for children who are keen to read different books but may lack motivation (particularly over long school holidays). Simply write down on a piece of paper, divided into six squares with a pencil and ruler, six types of books you would like them to read. For example, a book with a horse in it, a book about boats, a book that makes you happy, a spooky story. The aim is for them to find these books (libraries are great for this) and tick them off when they've read one. You could even make space in their bingo grid for them to briefly write about each book they choose.

SPECIAL WORD

This little hack is a lovely way of making reading a book together just a little bit more fun. Choose a 'special word', one that you know is in the book but will not come up too often. It could be the name of one of the characters, a place or an action. Every time they read with you and find that word in the book, the child has to do something silly, such as jump up and down three times or pat their head. Not only does this little trick make reading full of giggles, but it may also encourage children to read for longer and more often.

TAKING TURNS

When a child is reading aloud to an adult, they don't always have to read the whole book or text. To take the pressure off, you could share the reading, taking it in turns to read a paragraph each. This is also a nice tactic to use when children are getting tired of reading their reading book and becoming less motivated. To keep them feeling successful, you could help to finish off reading the last couple of pages for them and, over time, reduce the amount you read for them.

MAKE A BOOK CLUB

Discussing what they have read informally is great for children's comprehension skills (see the Introduction). To make this more exciting you could create a 'mini book club'. This could be at school or at home as a family, choosing an accessible book for everyone to read and then discuss. The aim is definitely not to put children under pressure to finish the book. Care needs to be taken to ensure it is achievable for the children to read the chosen book within the time frame. The purpose is for children to enjoy the social side of talking about books – what they loved about them, what happened, if they think the ending was fair and so on – developing that love of books that we want them to have.

USE THE 'TECH'

Embrace the technology available, for example, e-readers or e-book readers. These are simply electronic devices that you can read books on. Most smart phones now have applications that allow you to use your phone for this purpose too. The advantage of e-readers is huge, as they enable you to make text more accessible for children. You can change the font size, font colour, line spacing, background colour and much more. This can be brilliant for children who may require a different coloured background to read effectively (e.g. children who have the visual stress) or who have a visual impairment and need the text in a larger font. It's also useful for some dyslexic children, enabling them to have the options of a dyslexic-friendly font, bigger line spacing and larger text. You can also change the brightness of the screen to make it more comfortable to read.

ALL ABOUT AUDIO BOOKS

Listening to a story being read as opposed to reading it themselves may, at first glance, appear like a counter-intuitive suggestion when our aim is to improve children's reading, but bear with me. Audio books make books more accessible; they enable children to enjoy listening to a story that they might not be able to read yet. This is useful for many reasons. Not only does it help children fall in love with books and access stories that their peers might be reading but it also improves vocabulary.

Children can read along to audio books or read the book after they've listened to it, both of which help to build their confidence along the way. In addition, audio books can be helpful for comprehension tasks, as children can rewind to find the part of the text that a question asks them about. They help them focus on understanding the content of the book as opposed to reading the words. Importantly, audio books can give children independence, a new hobby and something to help pass the time on long journeys.

READER PENS

These are another helpful reading tool. They are particularly useful for helping children read short parts of text. Reader pens are small, discreet, pen-shaped technology that read out loud text that the child highlights. Some reader pens can also be used by some students in exams when they are older as a reasonable adjustment (if successfully applied for).

WRITE A REVIEW

A lovely activity you can do with children after reading a book is to write a review of it. This helps children to reflect on what they liked about it and what they might like to read next. Why not help them to write a real review on an online bookshop's website or even write a letter to the author? They could also choose to start a reading journal, jotting down brief reviews of each book they have read. These options give purpose not only to reading, but to their writing too.

READING NOOKS

Making an inviting space for reading both at home and at school can be a lovely way to encourage children to enjoy books. I'm by no means suggesting spending a lot of money on this; instead, involve the children in the task. They could, for example, make a reading den using an old sheet pegged onto a line and fill it with cushions and soft toys! Or make a space to read outside in the warmer weather using a rug to sit on and an umbrella for shade. Often if you let children take control of creating it, they have more ownership of the end result. I've seen some really clever reading areas in schools too, from beautiful school libraries with 'book vending machines' to cosy reading areas in classrooms.

VISIT A LIBRARY

Visiting the library or a book shop can be fantastic for igniting a love of reading. Not only are they often lovely, relaxing environments but they offer children the gift of *choice* when it comes to the books they would like to read. This is powerful. Children also have the opportunity to ask the real-life experts on books – librarians – for recommendations and advice when selecting one.

Most importantly, perhaps, by showing children that there are places completely dedicated to books, we are also demonstrating the *value* books have in our society.

WRITING HACKS

DOES IT NEED TO BE A PEN?

I don't know about you, but most of the writing I do isn't with a pen in hand...it's on my computer or tablet, typing away. If I'm honest, I'm not even sure I would have wanted to write this book if I'd have had to write it by hand! So why the push on pens? I'm not suggesting *all* children should type *all* the time and we should banish pens and pencils to the past. But if sometimes the objective of a task isn't to perfect their handwriting, then why not let them type? Why are we making it more difficult for them? These aren't 'cheats'; they not only remove the barriers that writing with a pen might have for some children with SEND (putting them on a more equal playing field) but also help children learn *how* to use the tools they may need to use when they are adults completing written work.

PEN PAL

Many children struggle to want to write because they don't see the purpose. It can sometimes feel as if they are writing for the sake of it. So, give them a reason! One such way is having a pen pal. Writing to someone can be a wonderful activity that encourages children to enjoy writing and reading. They could become 'pen pals' with a grandparent, for example, either via written letter or email. Be selective with pen pals to safeguard children, making sure they are a person you know and trust.

ENVELOPES AND STAMPS

Try to encourage writing in their play by setting up a little area with some envelopes, cards, note paper, an address book and even some stamps. Parents, you could even take your children with you to post letters and let them see you open your post (including those bills!). Sometimes children need to see *why* we write.

MAKE UP MNEMONICS

Mnemonics can be an excellent way for some children of remembering spellings. I still use some myself that I was taught at primary school. Simply put, it's when you assign a word for each letter of a word to make a memorable short sentence. It can be great fun to make up some mnemonics together for those tricky spellings they are learning. The sillier the better! Here are some of my favourite mnemonics:

- Because – big elephants can always understand small elephants.
- Does – dogs only eat sausages.
- Rhythm – rhythm helps your two hips move.
- Necessary – never eat cake eat salad sandwiches and remain young.
- Two – two wise owls.
- Said – small ants in danger.

NOTEPAD OR DIARY

Little notepads (even homemade) or diaries can be a nice way of encouraging children to practise writing in their own time. The trick is not adding any pressure, but by providing them with the tools to write and the space to do it, they may be inclined to have a little go. Diaries in particular can be fantastic for children to practise writing, as they only require children to write short snappy sentences about a topic they know lots about (themselves!).

START THE SENTENCE

A blank piece of paper can be extremely daunting for children. Sentence starters are a simple way of helping children get started with their writing. All you need to do is write the first bit of the sentence and leave it blank for them to continue.

MIND MAPS

Help children to organize their ideas for written work with mind maps. Write the title in the centre of a page and help them to write their key ideas around it. Children can then refer to it when they start writing.

HIGHLIGHTERS

One area that lots of children find tricky is comprehension tasks. These are where you need to read something and then use the information in the text to answer some questions. A simple hack to help with this is highlighter pens/underlining. Show children how to revisit the text, highlight the key bit it is asking about and then refer to it when writing the answer.

SPEECH-TO-TEXT SOFTWARE

For children who have difficulties with writing, sometimes it may be helpful to use technology such as speech-to-text software. This is software that records what they say and transcribes it onto a typed document. Using technology to help children with their writing doesn't just help them now, but provides them with useful strategies for when they are older too. There are many dyslexic adults who use speech-to-text software for all their written work.

ARE YOU SITTING COMFORTABLY?

There is a lot to think about when it comes to sitting comfortably to write, from thinking about the table height and if their feet are firmly on the floor, to their posture. Some children may also need slight movement when they are sitting, to enable them to concentrate better. For example, some children with ADHD find 'wobble cushions' useful. These are small cushions that can be sat on and help to improve posture, stability in their core muscles and enable them to move around a little bit. Other resources that can be helpful are weighted lap blankets, fidget toys and writing slants.

CHOOSE THE PEN

Do you have a favourite pen? I know I do. Writing with a special pen can make a difference to motivation as well as how it physically feels to write. If possible, let children choose their writing equipment and ensure it's comfortable to write with. If you notice children not holding their pencil correctly or comfortably when writing, have a look at helping them with their pencil grip. You could try using pencil grips, triangular/rectangular-shaped pencils or special handwriting pencils that have a built-in pencil grip.

PICTURE PROMPTS AND WORD MATS

Picture prompts can be a simple and useful resource to stimulate writing. All you need to do is print some pictures that relate to what they are writing about, to give them some idea of where to start. Word mats are usually an A4 sheet of paper with a collection of key words for the topic written on for them, sometimes with corresponding illustrations. These encourage independence for children who may need help with spelling certain words or remembering the key terms to include in their work.

FRIDGE MAGNETS

Popping some magnetic letters onto either a fridge at home or a whiteboard at school can be a really easy way of encouraging reading. It is also a great way for children to practise forming words and sentences. You could try leaving little messages to each other discreetly by organizing the letters (when they aren't looking) to form a sentence. They may enjoy the game of sneakily rearranging the letters to create a message back!

COMIC STRIPS

If children need to write a story or organize a series of events in some other written work, why not help them set it out as a comic strip to start with? They write a short summary sentence for each picture, in order, and can then use this to help them formulate paragraphs for their written work. Alternatively, they could write their key points on sticky notes to help organize their thoughts.

SCRIBE

Sometimes it may be necessary to scribe (write) for them for some tasks. This isn't 'giving up'; this is enabling children who find writing particularly difficult to feel the joy of getting their ideas on paper without the frustration of writing. This can be a great way of taking the pressure off and letting children enjoy learning. It may be that over time you are able to reduce the amount of written work you scribe for them.

STAND UP

Writing on an upright surface, standing up, can be helpful for some children. This could be on a clipboard, an easel, a big whiteboard or a clingfilm easel, as in activity 6 in Chapter 1. Not only can it be an easier way for some children to write who find writing on paper tiring but standing up to write can be really beneficial for developing gross motor skills that may ultimately help children when they are sitting down writing too! A win win!

WHITEBOARD

Mini whiteboards are a fun way for children to practise writing, and they can also be easier to write on as the dry-wipe pens are big and chunky and require very little pressure to make a mark. You can take a photo of their work on the whiteboard to keep it too. There's also the added bonus that children can erase their work more easily, reducing any anxieties over making mistakes. It's important, however, to be mindful of children who are left-handed, as when writing on whiteboards they may struggle to avoid rubbing off their work with their arm.

FINAL THOUGHTS

Thank you for taking the time to read my book. I hope you (and the children you teach or parent) have enjoyed trying out the play-based activities. My aspiration is that this will have helped to spark a love of reading and writing for the children in your care, that they will see literacy-based activities as fun, enjoyable and something to look forward to.

I know reading and writing are not easy for many children, and I hope that I've helped you to reflect on some of the barriers that the children in your care may face with literacy and to think about ways to tear these barriers down to make reading and writing accessible and enjoyable for all.

USEFUL RESOURCES AND RECOMMENDED READING

There are lots of fantastic resources out there to help you support children with their reading and writing, from websites and charities to books. I can't pretend, unfortunately, to know them all and there will be some that I will have missed. But as a starting point, here are some books and websites (including my own!) that you may want to look at to help:

Books

Botrill, G. (2018) *Can I Go and Play Now? Rethinking the Early Years*. London: Sage Publishing.

Bryce-Clegg, A. (2020) *365 Days of Play*. London: Sage Publishing.

Durrant, G. (2021) *100 Ways Your Child Can Learn Through Play: Fun Activities for Young Children with SEN*. London: Jessica Kingsley Publishers.

Kelly, K. and Phillips, S. (2011) *Teaching Literacy to Learners with Dyslexia: A Multi-sensory Approach*. London: Sage Publishing.

Lazarus, S. (2021) *ADHD is Our Superpower: The Amazing Talents and Skills of Children with ADHD*. London: Jessica Kingsley Publishers.

Goouch, K. and Lambirth, A. (2011) *Teaching Early Reading and Phonics: Creative Approaches to Early Literacy*. London: Sage Publishing.

Grant, D. (2017) *That's the Way I Think: Dyslexia, Dyspraxia, ADHD and Dyscalculia Explained*. London: Routledge.

Griggs, K. (2021) *This Is Dyslexia*. London: Vermilion.

Hultquist, A. (2013) *Can I Tell You About Dyslexia? A Guide for Friends, Family and Professionals*. London: Jessica Kingsley Publishers.

McNeil, J., Stone, R. and McNeil, P. (2021) *Mission Dyslexia*. London: Jessica Kingsley Publishers.

Muter, V. (2021) *Understanding and Supporting Children with Literacy Difficulties*. London: Jessica Kingsley Publishers.

Sandman-Hurley, K. (2019) *Dyslexia and Spelling: Making Sense of It All*. London: Jessica Kingsley Publishers.

The Spelling Rule Book (2009) Wakefield: SEN Marketing.

Reid, G. and Guise, J. (2019) *Assessment for Dyslexia and Learning Differences: A Concise Guide for Teachers and Parents*. London: Jessica Kingsley Publishers.

Rooke, M. (2017) *Dyslexia Is My Superpower (Most of the Time)*. London: Jessica Kingsley Publishers.

Charities, organizations and websites

www.addiss.co.uk
www.adhdfoundation.org.uk
www.ambitiousaboutautism.org.uk
www.autism.org.uk
www.barringtonstoke.co.uk
www.bdadyslexia.org.uk

www.cricksoft.com/uk/clicker
www.dekkocomics.com
www.doorwayonline.org.uk
www.driveryouthtrust.com
www.dyslexiashow.co.uk
www.dyslexiefont.com
www.dyspraxiafoundation.org.uk
www.ican.org.uk
www.nessy.com
www.noticeability.org
www.oakabooks.co.uk
www.ransom.co.uk
www.reachoutasc.com
www.readeasy.org.uk
www.readingeggs.com
www.ruthmiskin.com
www.senresourcesblog.com
www.sirenfilms.co.uk
www.studyingwithdyslexiablog.co.uk
www.succeedwithdyslexia.org
www.toe-by-toe.co.uk

INDEX

· · · · · · · · · · · · · ·